The Luckiest Dogs

By Cameron Macintosh

Pete’s Dog Place is a home for dogs and puppies that don’t have mummies or daddies.
Pete helps find homes for the dogs.

He gives them food, water and a safe place to sleep.
He plays with them every day, too!

Pete tries to find the dogs new families.

Pete's dogs are happy at his place, but they will be happier with a family.

Bren comes to see the puppies.

Bren chooses Milo, because Milo is the silliest puppy!

Bren laughs as Milo runs and jumps around the yard.

Tam likes fluffy dogs.

"This is Floss," says Pete.
"She's the fluffiest dog I have!"

"I love Floss!" cries Tam.
"She tried to lick my face!"

Jem wants a tiny dog.

"Pep is the tiniest dog here," says Pete.

"Then we'll take Pep home!"
Jem replies.

Pop would be happier with an older dog.

Duke comes to Pop for a pat.

Duke will be happiest getting hugs from Pop!

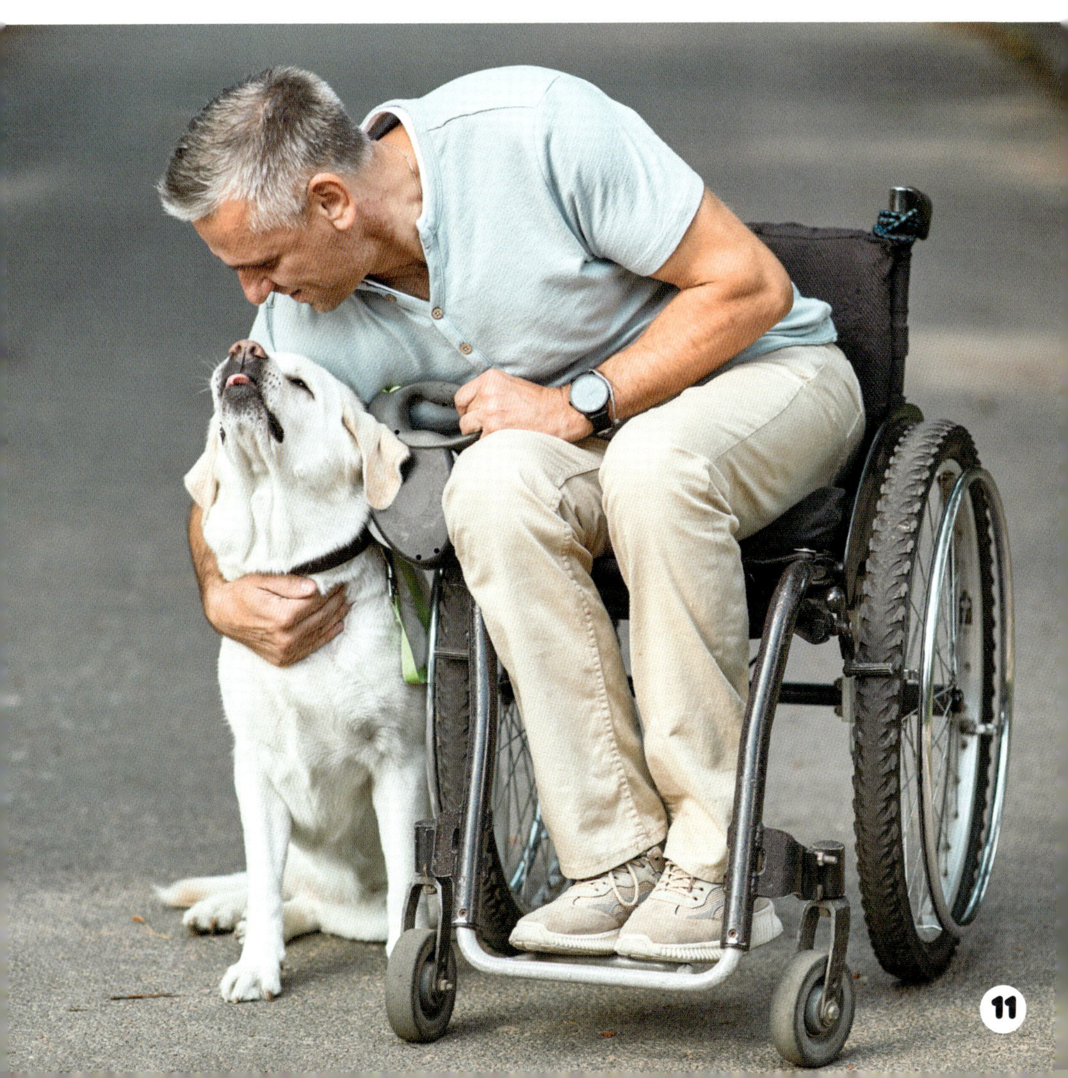

Josh studies all the dogs.

He does not know what kind of dog to get.

"I'm happiest when I'm sitting on the couch," Josh tells Pete.

"Then you will love Bob!"
says Pete.
"Bob is lazier than most dogs!"

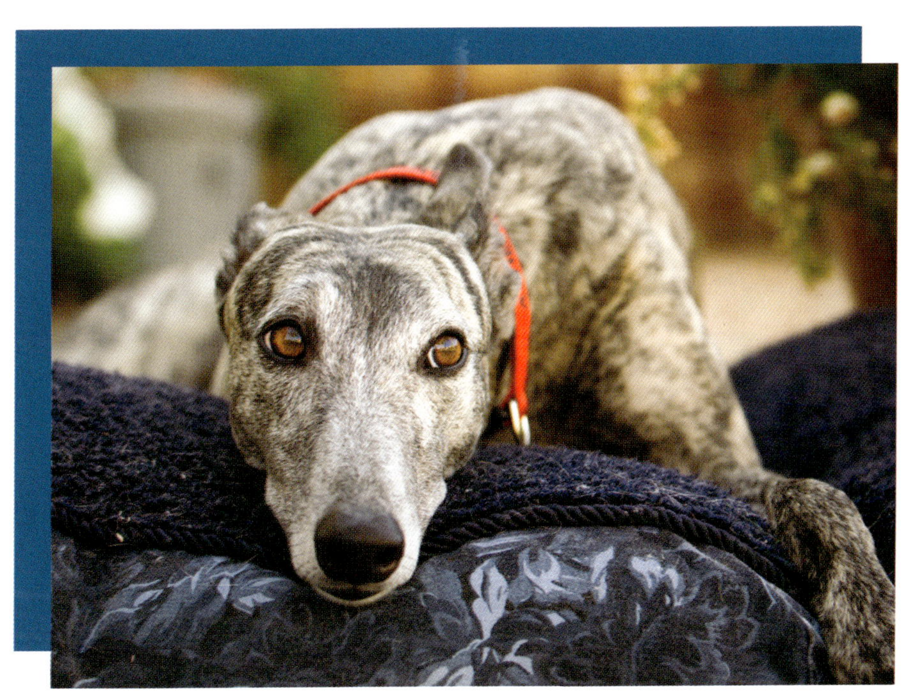

Pete's dogs are the luckiest dogs! He loves to match them with the best families.

CHECKING FOR MEANING

1. What sort of dogs does Tam like? *(Literal)*
2. Why does Pete think Josh will like Bob the dog? *(Literal)*
3. Why would Pop be happier with an older dog like Duke? *(Inferential)*
4. Does Pete do a good job at matching the dogs with their new families? Why? *(Evaluative)*

EXTENDING VOCABULARY

puppies	Look at the word *puppies*. What is the base of this word? How is the base changed to turn it into *puppies*? How does this change the meaning of the base?
fluffiest	What does it mean if something is the fluffiest? How might it look and feel? What is the fluffiest thing you can think of?
lazier	What is the base of the word *lazier*? What does it mean if someone is lazy? What does it mean if they are lazier? What word means "the most lazy"?

MOVING BEYOND THE TEXT

1. A puppy is a baby dog. What are some other words used for animal babies?
2. Why are places like Pete's Dog Place important?
3. Why should you tell an adult if you find a lost animal? Why should you leave it alone?
4. What are some words you would use to describe your ideal pet? Would it be a dog or another animal?

TIME TO WRITE

Write about your pet or a pet you would like to have. Describe what your pet looks like, what its personality is like and what you do with your pet.